Cocktails in the Wild

Poems by

Robert Knox

Copyright©2018 Robert Knox

All Rights Reserved

Published by Unsolicited Press

Image for cover provided by Robert Knox.

No part of this book may be reproduced or transmitted in any form or by any means without written permission from the publisher or author.

Printed in the United States of America.

Attention schools and businesses: for discounted copies on large orders, please contact the publisher directly.

ISBN: 978-1-947021-21-1

CONTENTS

I: Cocktails ... 1
    Invitation to the Feast ... 2
    The Wind Speaks Up ... 4
    But for the Art of it Alone ... 5
    Voluptuous ... 6
    The World Below ... 7
    After a Death ... 8
    The Rebel Angels Look Back (Goodbye to Florida) ... 9
    The Paradise of Birds ... 11
    Hay(na)kuSonnet:Cocktails on the Balcony ... 16

II. Wild Ideas ... 17
    From Out of the Inbox ... 18
    Sacred Cowers ... 20
    Election Season ... 23
    The Clock Maker ... 26
    Manticore ... 27
    Talking to India ... 29
    The Nightingale Role ... 32
    Holes at the Heart of Things ... 35
    My America (i) ... 37
    My America (ii) ... 40
    Twentieth Century Man ... 43
    You Had to Be There ... 45

ACKNOWLEDGEMENTS 47
About the Author 49

I: Cocktails

Invitation to the Feast

I'd like to start with Inspiration Soup. A small bowl if it's strong enough. I'm leaning to Puccini, and if you have something off "La Fanciulla del West," I'd be in emotional-culinary heaven.
(Add a dash of emoticon if you're of a mind to.)
If not the "Ch'ella mi creda," the tenor's fabulous heart-breaking Act III aria -- a classic Consommé of Tears -- then maybe something from the long love-duet at the start of Act II?
Always look for these items: love to eat my heart out.
After which the appetizer is surplus to nourishment. My appetite is fine: I'll have a glass of Rhyme Wine,
along with a lightly sautéed brain teaser: Couplets of the Immortality Ode, perhaps, served in a melancholy sauce.
Tempt me not with thy salads of Green Health. I've been down to the Salley Gardens, but it seems someone has left the Yeats open and the rabbits got in.
My taste runs more to savory-sour. If you have a blue cheese burger handy, remove everything but the blues. Add figs, maybe, and something sweet, sweethearts of artichoke will do.
Nothing meaty gets past me now. Smells arouse me, the scent of success on the plate: ribs of Old Adam, the sweetbreads of paradise, the laws of Italian sausage.
Is there a pasta course anywhere in this menu? Can I bowtie one on? I gknow a gnood gnocchi when I can gnaw one.
God, I forgot to order more wine. Bacchus will not be pleased.

Meet me in the garden afterwards,

and we'll share some dessert. How about "The Lineaments of Gratified Desire"? William Blake, c. 1795. A fine, old, slightly daring vintage.

The Wind Speaks Up

All day so quiet I can hear the pages turning
Rumble of a distant train, till the wind speaks up

The guitars of the mind let the season unwind
Rapture of the sacred heart when the wind speaks up

Defeated by digits, a web of blackouts
I rail at disobedient plastics till the wind speaks up

The gatherings of silence in the greenwood song
The humble bees cling to the blossom, the wind speaks up

I pace the graves of silence where the late birds fledge
The empty nest, the streambed dry till the wind speaks up

But for the Art of it Alone

      (after reading Philip Larkin)

But for the art of it alone,
he takes his wounds out of the closet
tries one on,
critiques the effect

But later, living
as we all do, some years (if we are lucky),
the withdrawals are quite sincere
like clothes that have gone through
the wash enough
not new, real, worn thin
at the stresses.

The fresh air, the words best chosen
of all the world
the lines shine, illumine
his world
put out the lamp

he laughs in the dark

Voluptuous

the scent of a first few drops of summer rain
on a world of hot pavement

the nexus of medieval voices
in universes of hollow stone

a stranglehold on a wire fence
by a herd of hungry runner beans

hibiscus, yellow-gold plateware,
insects sucking on butterfly bush blooms
purple as kings

the harvest-time betrayal
of the bee who stung me
and made me sing with pain

The World Below

    (at Tyringham Cobble)

Down below, in the cemetery, the churchyard,
nothing moves
All things small
and silent and permanent

We ascend for the view
The rocks that lift us survive from worlds
too old for questioning
Unprecedented: they are the precedents

We have climbed here before
Our standing unchanged, the season perfected
Each year leaning further to the edge
the steeple higher, the cemetery closer

After a Death

Anne strikes back at February
taking a hammer, whaling away at the ice
that sucks tight to the house like some glittering coral
of ravenous cold, reefing the house with winter

"Do you want to know what feels good?" she asks
after a loss, a contemporary loss,
that shocking preview of the sins of old age
"Pounding away with a hammer
at the ice,"
the ice, it may be, in your soul

In the morning, after a meager thaw,
the icicles are thick and unadorned
like drunks who have thrown up on themselves

The windows howl for their lovers
the one who is missing does not return

The Rebel Angels Look Back (Goodbye to Florida)

In the last days of winter,
when the turn of the season will not come in the month that trumpets
its arrival with leonine roar,
strutting its changeable hour, full of sound and fury,
because the poor earth below is still burdened with six-foot phalanxes
of cold, slow-frozen dirty walls that once were known, modestly, as
"sidewalks,"

when the soul finds no sweet release in jumping the time to come,
the whole graduated journey,
and so launch we (instead) tormented flesh straight to the days of eighty
in the shade,
sun-burnished sand beneath the toes,
warm saltwater sluicing the limbs
like the gurgling god of peripatetic Neptune, green and endlessly inventive,
palms being palms, swaying heavy-handed, lifted overhead in some
      unsolicited blessing,
familiar flowers looking like July,
creatures ordinarily clad stretched bare to the healing air

-- well, in brief, we'll take it,
balm and anodyne,
warm water, pleasant airs, fair breezes
and from the look of things (neighbors smiling like cream-fed cats)

nobody paying a dime for any of this

Till, thunder-struck on a summer's day,
time's fell hour slices down, our curtain falls and
villain check-out time, that winter of the imagination,
      looms before us,
we gather our share of remembrance to trundle northward,
icy patches sloughing beneath the wings of the homebound jet

And picturing once more, in the album of bittersweet remembrance
those beatitudes with attitudes, postures and beatific smiles of those who
recline as if forever on adjustable chairs in the rarefied green sleeves
of heavenly breezes, sunlit hours, occasional cloudiness, a few sprinkles
      just the other night
dampening the towels and yesterday's bathing suits,
contemplating the dip in the pool or the body-poach of the hot tub later,
supper on the balcony,

how could we not feel (if only for an instant)
like disobedient angels casting last looks at paradise lost
as they are driven cruelly to a very warm place
which frankly -- at certain times, days of blizzards, blackouts, and broken
      trains --
does not sound too very terrible either.

The Paradise of Birds

1.
It is not for everyone,
        this Paradise of Birds
The wingless ones who stand beneath the shade-cover
        on the boardwalk pavilion
Are given leave to watch,
a dozen brown and watery feet away,
the color of old trees glimpsed in a window's reflections,
bits of shell and water-eaten leafage at the base

We'll get no closer
The birds know how to measure distance --
        and ability, we have no wings to fly --
They land on a dime, on a dollar-sized island
We stand on ceremony,
the gnawing anxiety of wet feet,
as if water itself were toxic
We are lingering glances and superannuated vigilance,
but eyes cannot hurt them
We pose no threat to the Paradise of Birds

Who brings the stork's babies?
We question one another
A head like the curve of an umbrella handle

      turned upside down,
The wood stork is patterned silk on top,
yards of plump white plumage below
Its young both indescribable and hard to glimpse

Not half-brown like the Anhinga,
whose adolescents are caramel feathered
and bear their allegiance to a race of beige and mustard-colored snake people
and live below the waters now
in a world we cannot see
We satisfy our craving for vision with the Paradise of Birds

Birds, we know, are merely people
      in a different dress
(Cannot the same be said of trees?)
They too enjoy a fine March day
in the face of a smiling sun, fish a-plenty
(Where we live no such days exist)
They toy with the furniture inside their nests,
adjust the framing, smooth the slipcovers,
content to ignore the squawks of the babes
      demanding to be fed

They are beyond such needs
      in weather like this --
pellucid, clear as glass, free of insects and parasites,

holding wings high to dry in the sun
like Washing Day in some earlier time
(though without the elbow grease)
all pleasure, no work

They are nature's machines for turning air and water
        into the grace of flight
that miracle of which we are always bereft,
banned forever from the Paradise of Birds

The herons, winged heroes, glitter-glide beside the people,
aging creatures who crave to worship
        in the glow of their beauty
Who will fly only when they leave
        this heavier career behind one last time,
for good (seeking entrance then
        to the Paradise of Birds)

Who fly only eyes closed, limbs inert
in the phantasms of the liberated chambers of the brain,
        those rooms they cannot decorate or conform to will
Who soar only in their minds,
        their mind's eye of stimulus and love
Who gaze with longing, and
        wonder
at the Paradise of Birds

2.

Only one beast disturbs the Paradise of Birds
It syncopates the water
       in brownish segments
a disturbance in the watercolor
       as if old paint got up to walk

It motors in silence,
like appetite
or time, or the silent renewal of
       solid earth beneath your feet
Arrives like surprise
Like thought made visible,
an idea given shape
Like Hegel's notion of history
a submerged and troubled mass forming for revolt

Yet subtle as a reptile
Its metrics are known
by the clear-eyed cousins roosting
       in the bare tops of the cypress trees,
those skeletal frames and furniture
       for the Paradise of Birds

And when the stick-legged guardians of heaven, their rapiers
       in their faces,
their light and parried weaponry

tied snuggly to their brains

They hoot their worries, in airy syncopation,

a ceaseless one-two-three,

warning all of the creature's trespass,

the reptile in the sally garden waters
        of the Paradise of Birds

Hay(na)kuSonnet: Cocktails on the Balcony

Beirut
One flag
Three green peoples

March
Two movements
under the sun

Borders
Israel, Syria
One tough neighborhood

History
Cedars, alphabet
Bring back Phoenicia

With Mediterranean view
Drinks on you

II. Wild Ideas

From Out of the Inbox

I delete the forty-two solicitations for campaign donations
from the little people
to combat the rivers of invisible money spewed
by the other side's billionaires
Our billionaires apparently are not so fluent

We are 'the little people'
I see us hurrying off to work
carrying our battered briefcases, umbrellas exploding in
the storms of autumn, freezing our tushes
on the frozen sidewalks in the winter of the century,
scampering beneath the heavy boots
and skyscraper legs of the corporate storm-troopers

Why can we fight money only with more of the same?
Why can't we donate paper flowers,
old Valentines with crayoned kisses, children's report cards with
the A's circled, clever bowls of kale salad
the smiles of knee-high nieces coaxed by frequent application
of sugary liquids,
pencil-worn scorecards with the names of diamond idols
seen now only in the studio wrap-up
lamenting that hanging slider in the top of the seventh?

Why does the permanent political class
expect to get paid when the only interest
served by marathon campaign carnivals
that crowd the air with Ferris wheels of denigration
and roller-coasters of paid duplicity
is their own?

I walk in a garden of video promises
digital invitations with sticky fingers
breath-taking ascents to rhetorical prospects where the air is thin
transitory surveys, singular snapshots of
a moving stream of media eventualities

in which we float, we little people,
on folded paper boats carrying our little piles
of GW's portrait, we pioneers of *vox populi percuniae*
praying for pennies from heaven
when the rainbow coalition is enuf

Sacred Cowers

American shibboleths:
the arthritic sclerotic idolized Constitution, the all too semi-sovereign
        states,
the short-circuited electrical college,
those doddering fools squatting on an ancient panel of archons supreme:
Rule by anachronism

Oh no, what would our founding fathers say?
(No 'mothers,' notice:
might that tell you something?)
As if Genesis were your science book:
In the beginning the documentarians created the heavens
and the Second Amendment, and the everybody-gets-two, big or small,
Romanesque Senate
And the three-fifths rule to protect the peculiar institution
('peculiar' doesn't begin to cover it)
And what would the framers say about their original intent
to permit no abridgment of our natural right to buy a cruise missile
at a gun show to better impress our enemies at the high school?

Who dares scorn the special madness of aMErica?
"The pure products of America go crazy, "wrote William Carlos Williams
who worried about "imaginations which have no/

peasant traditions to give them/
character"
I too prefer peasants to certain characters
who strut their hour under the TV lights
papering bankrupt palaces with tissues of lies

It's American traditions that worry me:
Shoot first and ask questions later
Fear the face of the black man
relying on your badge and your whiteness as a license to kill

Where are the law-givers and truth-tellers
Who refuse to pledge allegiance to
our immaculate conception by Constitution
a document frankly framed in fearful compromise
when hardly anyone could vote,
'persons' were totaled at a discount to pacify slave-holders
but had no rights, not even to life
loaded muskets were stacked by the door in fear
of Indian raids or slave revolts
California was regulated by mission bells
Texans were under the innocent impression they were Mexicans
and the conquest of Canada just a matter of time?

I say level the anachronistic states, flatten the field,
play clean with democracy,
let the computers do the math: one person, one vote across the board,

the majority empowered to form conclusions, make laws, and depose old Uncle Moneybags from the ruling bench in favor of a posse of wise women, an Alaskan shaman, and the personal appointee of the Dalai Lama

Election Season

Jesus announces
the perfect candidate
no past, no digital footprint, no peccadilloes on record
a few snide comments on the rich,
but they'll get over it

His cabinet is not of this world
His program does more with less
gathering the crumbs, applying funny math
to balance the food budget,
fuzzy logic to save one baddie,
let the citizens beyond reproach fend for themselves
(or cast the first stone)
His paradoxical predictions
always sound good,
though nobody understands what he's saying
That's good too because (his handlers tell us)
don't criticize what you can't understand

His ratings ascend,
supporters flock to his appearances,
dropping their tools to
climb to the rally on the mount,
seeking love in all the high places

They give whatever they can't hide overseas to the poor
and follow him
He speaks of hope, of mysteries, of paradox
of lovable neighbors
His disciples march on the capital
The people, they chant, want the fall of the regime

But the regime is a criminal empire
with a knack for skewering rebels
The oligarchs have more money than sense
They work the back channels, intrigue for no reason,
draw scandals in the air
False witnesses are recruited to demand his retraction
The perfect candidate is humiliated, scapegoated,
They pile rumors upon him,
bear him down with microphones
Even then we love him
The chains are our own, but he wears them so well

Banished, to a better place,
We can't see him any more
But we know he's there
It's a miracle, but also a deal
He gets his reputation back, but stays out of politics

A millennium goes by, and then a second
New money comes to the neighborhood

They fix up Harlem, gentrify the flooded wards
of the city beneath the sea,
The wheel turns, the bubble rises,
deflates, come up some ways again,
like the mercury in spring

After many years the wanderer from the wilderness,
a simple man, perhaps a fool,
revisits the capital, registers the fresh paint
and the spruced-up storefronts
Among the poor he can discern no change

The Clock Maker

The Deus who made the universe
was a clock-maker,
an intricate machine, both macro and micro,
he wound it up, then set it going

Eons later, a boy finds a way to measure
how things go,
he brings his invention to school,
an institution that conducts him kindly to a police car

to show him, and all the rest of us,
how this world runs.
Deus wept

Manticore

September heat
Huge mantises copulating on the butterfly tree
Monarchs beware!

They prey, all right
They linger on the buddleia
waiting for the butterflies to hone in
on something that smells like home
but home, in their case, is The End

'He' catches 'her' there one day
even though she's twice his size,
and though at times she has spread her limber length
across the bay window,
like some beastie escaped from a mad-scientist matinee
stalking some artificial sanctuary
for the winged protein that is her meat

Too big for squeamish hands to touch
too raw for greenleaf thoughts of preservation
too distinguished in her regicidal enormity to ignore
though her body swims meta-morphically into the green and brown
of everyman's little spot of paradise

Serpentine in her motions

she knows what we don't care to hear

Let the gods, the *elohim*, keep track of the billion teeming souls of creation

I step away, indulge a somewhat less sullied patch of sun

As for the guy on her back,

if he's runt enough, he's lunch

Talking to India

I try to remember how to say the Indian word --
Sanskrit? is that still around? --
for 'corpse pose,'
my favorite moment in yoga class,
as if, somehow, I can't wait to be dead
(actually I can, thanks, in case anyone with authority in these matters
is listening in)
which is spelled *savasana* (though
(pronounced *Sha*-vasana),
making me think of Sha NaNa (whose lead singer I once interviewed)
Remembering this sublime conjunction of sound and body
sometimes, forgetting often,
I should not be shocked, therefore,
when the Indian man on the corporate help-line
mispronounces 'premises,' saying something like "pre-*mee*-ses"
making the word sound like some sort of
bodily byproduct,
which I am certain is not his intention

'Do you have any pets on your pre-*mee*-ses?'
'Why do you wish to know?'
'Do you have any security codes, or fences on your pre-*mee*-ses?'
'Do you mean my place of residence?'
I explain where the accent belongs,

we share the complicated laugh

of travelers arriving at the same respite from different journeys,

but then it is back to the Land of Cross Purposes

I wish to lay my consumer's wrath at the doorstep

of *somebody* taking up space in the USA

Alas, he knows no person who fits this description

nor possesses any phone number for his (presumably American) company

in my country

In the Age of Digitalia

our connections are fouled at the mind's borders

my urge to rage against the corporate masters,

deflected, sublimated, ultimately blunted by their desire to remain secure,

    inviolate, impervious

behind the virtual separation wall

of the inevitably dispiriting eight-hundred number

and the voices hired to know nothing of *them*

and everything of *you* that can be put into a number

Someday, my nameless friend, you may come to this great country of ours,

and see for yourself the condition of my *prem*-ises

but you will surely be disappointed

by the absence of codes, of security, and barriers

the utter dearth of four-legged creatures with sharp teeth,

vicious claws and whining voices

that bark or hiss in English

and likewise when I stumble off the plane

to visit that great country of yours, I will look here and there,

high and low

and nowhere discover that perfect place

where I may lay my tired bones

and discover the ultimate meaning of *savasana*

The Nightingale Role

Keats had it wrong
'no full-throated ease'
The nightingale isn't playing some hide and seek dalliance
with darkness and light in the universe
And we are wrong, misguided at least,
to focus on the beauty of his urgent song --
for, of course, it's the male who sings,
one of nature's great tenors
(if needed, we will find two others).
The nightingale sings it, as profoundly, soul-stirringly as he can,
because he is auditioning for the greatest role
either art or nature can provide him,
advertising his aptitude for male parentage.
The male nightingale, learned biologists tell us,
is "essential to the nest,"
not only to guard the young when the greedy beaks of the nestlings
squawk their insatiable hunger
but to feed the female during the days and weeks of incubation.

Let us be clear: they are 'providers.'
We heavy-footed, earthbound creatures know this role,
we call it 'Dad'
and it well describes my own good father, and maybe your Dad too,
but (frankly, babe) it sure ain't me.

Am I the only bird out there
who never liked this deal?
So, no patch on the nightingale perhaps, though in my time
I spread my wings over our nest
and kept a Wiffle bat handy to fend off home-invaders
and occasional stray bats of the winged rodent variety

and though I regularly feed my mate,
not only when new life is on the way,
but when she comes home late from work, plus
that strained after-hours flocking busy execs must fly to,
unerringly, bits of straw in their mouths in token
of their loyalty to some clawed presence in the catbird seat

... with rice and stir-fry waiting on the stove
and a ready ear for the tired post-mortem,
an open wing, and a bit of a song for smoothing feathers.

But 'provider' is a role I gladly yield
to the stalwart singer of the nightingale songs
those lambent jug-a-jugs, those dying falls and grace notes,
those arias of longing and entreaty
I do my singing,
for whose ears I never know
(my own? some other unknown presence
in the night?)

But as for 'providing,' darling,
a wise bird looks after herself.

Holes at the Heart of Things

("*Cosmologists Discover How Black Holes Can Leak.... Extra dimensions should allow information to escape from black holes, according to a new model of cosmology*" -- MIT Technology Review)

We stare into the skies
We ask our questions of the stars
We learn that life is the product of newly discovered nano-particles
called ribosomes,
25 million of which can fit into the period at the end of this sentence.

We've been asking the wrong people,
Talking to heavenly bodies, objects we can, in some sense of the term, 'see'
We're barking up the wrong tree-diagram
We should ask the dripping dark holes of matter who we are
We should ask *them*,
utterly other, laughing up their subatomic sleeves,
waiting for us to catch on

We find our predicament fascinating,
(hard to see, sometimes, why else we go on with it)
But we will never escape it
We cannot stop asking questions that, reason tells us, we'll never answer,
said the dummy to the wooden man

Pinocchio knows as much as we do, ultimately speaking
We study the things of this world,
the birds, and the trees, the creatures we love
(and some we do not love; not going there)
(mosquitoes, cancer cells: went there after all)
And lo, to our stunned and stupefied inspection
they grow ever more astonishing as our eyes get bigger,
our lenses drill ever more deeply into the interstices of the void,
but still they live in *our* world,
part of nature, part of us

We've been looking for truth in all the wrong places
Ask the electrons who we are
Ask the particles, slipping sub-microscopically through dripping dark
holes, exactly who we are

My America (i)

("There died a myriad... For *a botched civilization*" -- Ezra Pound)

Looking at you these fallen days (or me in the mirror)
I join the ranks of your disappointed admirers
We are no longer saving the world
we are saving our jobs
Frankly, I am sick of the whole 'greatest country in the world'
chest-thumpery
and if there were somewhere else to go I would go there
but (still true) if you are not part of the solution
you are part of the problem
and I know which part I am

America, my transcendental gender-free inamorata, you are my sole
        support
I am one of your pensioned ex-lovers, as glimpsed
in the film version of what-we-now-really-are,
walking the boardwalk
somewhere desolate, like Atlantic City,
the New Jersey Crimea, sucking up air like one of Chekov's washed-up
        emigres,
after the rodeo, after the gold rush, after the film festival, the short-series
        Conventions,
after the failed uprising, after the media has packed up and gone home

to spend a quiet evening in the hotel with their phones

one of your disappointed vampires in need of a bloody fix,
scanning the pre-dawn streets for Ginsberg set-piece atrocities,
the best minefields of America, dodging gunned-up, hyped-up,
trumped-up scaredy-cops shooting black men because we are afraid
of black men (why shouldn't we be? given all we have done to them?)
and are of course still doing with fanny-pats of approval
from race-card Republican judges

America, ghoulish dreamboat, ancient lover gone in the teeth,
eager for wounds to lick cuz you like the taste
you grow comfortable with the deaths of others
They are dying in Aleppo
Other countries (nursing their own broken mirrors) ask,
"What are they are thinking in America?"
They are not thinking in America
Thinking is not done in America,
some calculation of course, some texting, some advertising,
some truly boorish emoting
It's always about us, isn't it?
If not, then why are you bothering me?

My America! after the big affair, after the ball is over,
your kick-line of sulky dwarfs cleaning up behind the parade
You were young once
We were all young once

Your bright young men wore wigs and tight pants, showed a leg
Ladies learned to smoke, swear, dance and dip to apocalyp-stick swingtime
America, your century is over
You open your faded arms to tin pot dictators,
make eyes at banana republics, don the latest looks from funhouse mirrors,
worship pigs who despise everything you ever stood for

... all for a botched democracy, a menopausal male
gone grouchy in the knees, stiff in the frontal lobe
You have no use for carping critics
who spend time spooning with their buddy Google,
the single pop culture lightweight who can stand their company
Write me a check and I'll get out of town

My America (ii)

My America, however, is a guy with a distinctly 'different' name
that is to say clearly not Anglo-Saxon (a tongue with more than enough
    funny names of its own),
for example banjo player 'Bela Fleck'[1]
combining Hungarian roots with the Appalachian mountain music that
    now defines his instrument,
itself a melding of deep-flowing currents, Celtic, English, African-
    American
Who travels to Africa to trace the banjo's genealogy
in hide-covered stringed instruments brought here by slaves
In the film* you can see the respect in his eyes as his fingers work to copy
a finger-picking rhythm pecked at hummingbird speed by a Malian guitar
    player
and the respect in the eyes of the African players of the *akonting*
(a three-stringed, long-necked banjo antecedent)
as they see what Fleck can do with the modern version

The country, that is, of Yo-Yo Ma, Lang Lang, my Quincy neighbors
whose grandfathers visit to play basketball with preschool grandsons,
the lady who shouts with the half-dozen words we share that I have
planted my garden in the wrong place. 'What are these?' she points.
    'Nothing to eat?'

---

[1]"Throw Down Your Heart," 2008

The country of my wife's grandfather Meier who escaped the czar's army
to carry a sewing machine to work in Brooklyn
My close-mouthed father, born here in unlucky times,
who never once in our hearing spoke a word of his Depression childhood,
but survived to give us what he lacked and carried his secrets to the grave
The Nisei soldiers who stormed up mountains in Italy to take Nazi forts
while their parents were interned somewhere in the ambivalently 'Great'
    Plains,
and those with names like DiMaggio whose mothers were forced to
    register each year
as enemy aliens and whose travel-restricted fathers could no longer visit
    their sons' restaurants
while they fought in Europe and the Pacific
Of citizen Khizr Khan, whose officer son died protecting those who served
    under him in Afghanistan,
a country much like this one in having too many wars. (My America can
    be improved.)
And Zarif Khan, who founded an Afghani community in of all places
    Wyoming,
by taking advantage of a collection of opportunities
such as the ranch-hands' pent-up demand
for fresh tamales, the stock market, freedom of travel, the right to vote,
found perhaps nowhere else but in these United States

Of Darlene Love who went from house cleaner, to backup singer, to
    contributing

"Christmas (Baby Please Come Home)," to the nation's permanent
> holiday playlist

The country where an author (Barbara Ehrenreich)
could write a book titled "Nickel and Dimed: On (Not) Getting By in
> America"

and not be hounded by Putin's police
Of Cesar Chavez, Joan Baez, Sonia Sotomayor, Roberto Clemente, Rita
> Moreno

A country of 'climbing-up' ordinary heroes, open minds, thinkers and
> doers, money makers and music makers

with names our own Moms and Dads never heard of,
but learned to play nice with for the good of the whole, e pluribus unum
transcending the clans and tribalisms that set other worlds on fire
because we were the others, the strangers, the newcomers once, the
> genuine alien nation

Twentieth Century Man

Lawrence, death haunted your days
The last of the brood, the baby of the family when your father died
Leaving behind unrequited syndicalist longings in another tongue,
    the tongue of your childhood
You might have loved him, but you did not know him
Your brother, the true man of the family, the family that loved and
    cherished you,
        disappeared high over the Pacific
Closer to the angels or the eye of God than mortal life could bear
They called him "missing," but a smart kid in uniform knew what that
    meant
A nickel got you a subway ride back to Mom's or a ferry ride from the
    Charon who serviced Staten Island
Mom was old when you came back from the war,
enraging you with her unprovoked decline
When your sister took her shopping for relief of the feet and the shop girl
    talked her into sensible shoes
she declared to all humanity (in the language of her childhood)
 "Now you can say I'm an old lady"
No one wants to be old, but in those days not so many made it to the place
    where 'old' seems like the better choice
But you did, Lawrence, survivor, fortunate son,
there are you happy

When your embittered sister, some viper slipping between her
and her heart,
the last of your siblings
Died that summer, the weight of the ages shifted, the scales tipped,
What were you holding onto but your fear?
You faith countenanced no second act, no leaning together
for an ageless photo in the bleached sheaths
of some inter-generational heavenly Seder

Lawrence, I do you wrong
Every life sheds its quota of departures
(Count the heads and you'll know how many)
You shouldered your losses and forward marched
Lifting your little piece of the world
On love's back and holding it longer than even (no, especially) you
       thought possible
Now rest yourself, father, sit you down
All souls ride together on the journey to last things

You Had to Be There

When people like you were killed
having made the mistake of being born in the wrong place,
to the wrong people, doing poorly on their SATs
Even the winners, a chemistry major from Boston
dying forty-five years later when Agent Orange,
reports for duty: he was There
Or there, back then, in Central Park when the chanting stopped
No teargas, no riots, mere ceremonies of innocence
though later we get caught with a jay in the wrong place
by men with bulges on their belts and short haircuts
My girl sits on the evidence, our leader swallows the pill bag,
grunting answers, dulling the hunt for the hunters,
who shoe us off, fortunate white kids, to be there somewhere else
still Manhattan though, mid-town, then uptown
to a birthday party at the Statue of Alice

All of us still in Wonderland, milling on the town green
The National Guard showing up in fancy dress, four dead, white kids too,
but there in the wrong place when the unpredictable electrons
of a chance-driven universe coalesced into high-pressured lead
Black kids too, there in Mississippi, somehow tokened out of the story line
No longer to be anywhere// ever again// just like that.
But you had to be there,
that was the whole point, we were counting on you

Being anywhere else was irrelevant, virtually non-being
Here? No longer any good, time's dustbin, moldering color snaps
you clean from the basement when the old folks pass,
glean a few, mostly dispose
You had to be there// to understand
When the workers take down the show, roll up the maps, dethrone the
prints
from the wall, wipe the dust from the tapestries
To know what was real beyond love and regrets,
and to laugh in the right places,
you had to *be there*

ACKNOWLEDGEMENTS

Aubade Magazine published:
"The Clock Maker" and "Manticore"

Verse-Virtual.com published:
"Invitation to the Feast", "Voluptuous", "The World Below", "Hay(na)ku Sonnet: Cocktails on the Balcony", "After a Death", "From Out of the Inbox", "Sacred Cowers", "Election Season", "Talking to India", "The Nightingale Role", "Holes at the Heart of Things", and "Twentieth Century Man".

Yellow Chair Review published:
"The Wind Speaks Up"

Scarlet Leaf Review published:
"The Rebel Angels Look Back (Goodbye to Florida)," and "The Paradise of Birds."

The Somerville Times and *Misfit Magazine* published:
"You Had to Be There"

About the Author

A resident of Quincy, Massachusetts, Robert Knox is a freelance correspondent with a thousand bylines in the Boston Globe, writing about the arts, books, the environment, Massachusetts history, and the workings of governments. With an academic background in philosophy (Yale) and literature (Boston University) and years of journalistic experience, he brings a wide variety of interests to his poetry and fiction.

A contributing editor for the online journal Verse-Virtual.com, his poetry appears online every month. His previous chapbook "Gardeners Do It With Their Hands Dirty" received praise from other poets, including Robert Wexelblatt who said, "Knox's well-tended garden of verses furnishes readers with elegant borders, unexpected vistas, gorgeous blossoms, and insights as sharp as thorns. His themes are as local as the backyard and as universal as the weather."

His poems have also appeared in periodicals such as Guide to Kulchur Creative Journal, The Poetry Superhighway, Party, & Disaster Society, Off the Coast, Misfit Magazine, and others.

A fiction writer with stories in many publications, he published his first novel "Suosso's Lane," based on the Massachusetts roots of the infamous Sacco-Vanzetti case, in 2015. Reviewers praised the book. Novelist Patry Francis, author of "The Orphans of Race Point," called it "a beautiful novel, written with compassion, journalistic balance, and a deep sense of justice."

A prize winner in the Words With Jam short fiction contest, his story "Marriage" was published in the resulting anthology, An Earthless Melting Pot. After being named a Finalist in the Massachusetts Artist

Grants Program, excerpts from his story "Lost" appeared on the Mass Cultural Council website.

Drawing on his background as a reporter, columnist, and book reviewer, as well as his interest in gardening, nature, history, theater, photography, and politics, Knox is an active blogger at blog prosegarden.blogspot.com

www.ingramcontent.com/pod-product-compliance
Lightning Source LLC
Chambersburg PA
CBHW080028130526
44591CB00037B/2710